Praise for *Mend*

"Kwoya Fagin Maples's personae poems stun. Voiced such that we may not look away, *Mend* is a startling, stomping debut. Maples's masterful image-making magnetizes and mesmerizes. But *Mend* is no dreamland to drift through—it's a searing spotlight on a gruesome cog in the wheel of America's past. It's a litany of beautifully rhythmical and perfectly crushing poems. Art hurts and it heals. Kwoya Fagin Maples is a visionary doctor. History is humbled in her hands."

—Abraham Smith, author of *Destruction of Man*

"Kwoya Fagin Maples says it plain: 'bodies above virtue are never black.' In her debut collection, *Mend*, here is a black southern poet and mother explicitly calling out the lineage from which she descends—we are both haunted and healed by history. Maples's poems are narrative-driven, yet clear-voiced and lyrical; she writes us a world, a history, with her vision and leans back into a past to write herself into the story while rendering the abuses to the black woman's body in the name of science, and calls out: 'There's suffering here.' We hold our own breath through each sonnet sequence, each prose poem, until we understand, like Maples does, that the black mother's body is 'an aching shell . . . but . . . worth tenderness.'"

—DéLana R. A. Dameron, author of
Weary Kingdom: Poems

"Ancestral women whose strengths and humiliations have too long been lost to history, and contemporary women writing and revising their own storylines spring to vivid life vigorously imagined, vibrantl[y]

poems. Maples does not flinch to enunciate the disgusting truths of racism and misogyny; neither does she neglect the possibility of beauty. These poems carry an unbearable weight of witness: so much suffering, but also the joy of survival, the survival of joy. Open the door, enter 'the backyard of things past telling,' and be mended."

—Joel Brouwer, University of Alabama

Mend

Mend

Poems

Kwoya Fagin Maples

UNIVERSITY PRESS OF KENTUCKY

Scholarly publisher for the Commonwealth,
serving Bellarmine University, Berea College, Centre College of
Kentucky, Eastern Kentucky University, The Filson Historical Society,
Georgetown College, Kentucky Historical Society, Kentucky State
University, Morehead State University, Murray State University,
Northern Kentucky University, Transylvania University, University of
Kentucky, University of Louisville, and Western Kentucky University.
All rights reserved.

Editorial and Sales Offices: The University Press of Kentucky
663 South Limestone Street, Lexington, Kentucky 40508-4008
www.kentuckypress.com

Library of Congress Cataloging-in-Publication Data

Names: Maples, Kwoya Fagin, 1982– author.
Title: Mend : poems / Kwoya Fagin Maples.
Description: Lexington, Kentucky : The University Press of Kentucky,
[2018] |
   Series: The University Press of Kentucky New Poetry and Prose Series.
Identifiers: LCCN 2018021884 | ISBN 9780813176277 (pbk. : alk.
paper) | ISBN 9780813176284 (pdf) | ISBN 9780813176291 (epub)
Classification: LCC PS3613.A665 A6 2018 | DDC 811/.6—dc23
LC record available at https://lccn.loc.gov/2018021884

Member of the Association of University Presses

For the women—mamas. Your heat, your light—astounds.

The peculiarities in diseases of negroes are so distinctive that they can be safely and successfully treated, as a general rule, only by southern physicians, with a southern education.

—Advice among Masters:
The Ideal in Slave Management in the Old South

I am too pure for you or anyone.
Your body
Hurts me as the world hurts God. I am a lantern—

My head a moon
Of Japanese paper, my gold beaten skin
Infinitely delicate and infinitely expensive.

Does not my heat astound you! And my light!
All by myself I am a huge camellia
Glowing and coming and going, flush on flush.

—Sylvia Plath, *Fever 103°*

Contents

Preface   xi

I.

The Door   3
Mt. Meigs Arrival   6
The Doctor Asks If I Want to Go Home the Way I Came   7
Today the Doctor Says He Will Be Gingerly   8
Wool Door   9
A Thousand Cats   11
Unfolded   12
To Bear Witness   13
Belonging   14
Delia   15
So Familiar He Is with Parting Her Brown Legs   17
Dog in the Hospital 18
Sometimes I Think I Should Have Stayed Where I Was At   19
Fresh Sheet   20

II.

Oak, Pine, Basswood   24
Silk Umbrella, Dancing Pumps   25
Mary Catherine Is a Defeathered Chicken   26
Wild and Forbidding   27
I Can't Seem to Get to Mt. Meigs   28

III.

Prayer Meeting   31

The Orange   32

Overseer Story (Told with a Smile)   33

Delia   34

Elegy for a Stillborn: To the One Who Carries Him Away   35

Southern Pastoral   37

The Milk Still Comes In   39

Delia   40

I Could Never Disremember the Fireflies   41

Moon   42

Just Like the Light of God   43

I've Got Life   44

What Yields   46

Invention   58

IV.

Blueberry Poem   61

Meeting Anarcha   62

Brief, Terrific Rainstorms   64

For Dorothy Lorena Davis   65

Her Knife: Elegy for Dorothy Lorena Davis   67

This Poem Resists with Joy   69

Teeth   70

My Mother Bathes Me after I Give Birth   71

Acknowledgments   73

Notes   77

Bibliography   79

Preface

Between 1845 and 1849, Dr. James Marion Sims of Mt. Meigs, Alabama, performed experimental gynecological surgery on enslaved women who suffered from fistula (severe vaginal tears) due to difficult childbirth. Since fistula occurs as a result of prolonged labor, it can be safely assumed that most of the newborns died. We are only given three of the women's names in Sims's autobiography, *The Story of My Life*, which is referenced and quoted in this collection: Anarcha, Betsey, and Lucy. However, at least eleven women were experimental subjects at Mt. Meigs. Sims built a crude hospital behind his home where he housed these women—mothers—who were in hope of being cured. After a series of unsuccessful surgeries, Sims declared he had successfully repaired the injuries of one woman, Anarcha, who underwent a recorded thirty surgeries. After publishing his findings, he achieved the recognition he desired and became known as one of the first American doctors to conduct groundbreaking work in the field of gynecology. There are monuments dedicated to Sims in Alabama, South Carolina, and New York. Gynecologists today still use devices he developed, the most famous being the Sims speculum.

This collection is concerned with the lives of the women who were subjected to his experiments. The following poems are imagined memories and experiences told from the women's hospital beds. The poems also seek to reflect the fact that they were all addicted to opium.

Dear reader, here is my wish: that you would consider how this story relates to now. Presently in 2018, black women are three times more likely to die after childbirth than white women, regardless of ability to pay and regardless of prenatal care. Biases toward black bodies still exist within the medical profession that lead to such an imbalance in medical care. Fistula is still pervasive in impoverished countries, and women who suffer from it are often ostracized by their families and communities. Maybe, reader, with further consideration, you will see how you are connected with this story. Maybe you will honor what you come to know by sharing it.

I.

The Door

a naked
      woman
on knees
and hands
      in the backyard of things past telling

her odor
closing the space
      he taps apart her inner
thighs
her used
belly
   hangs
      like a sow's

then two new
      pewter spoons
and she knows
      she's not here
for mending

"Betsey, I told you that I would send you home this afternoon, but before you go I want to make one more examination of your case." She willingly consented. I got a table about three foot long, and put a coverlet upon it, and mounted her on the table, on her knees, with her head resting on the palms of her hands. I placed the two students, one on each side of the pelvis, and they laid hold of the nates, and pulled them open. Before I could get the bent spoon handle into the vagina, the air rushed in with a puffing noise, dilating the vagina to its fullest extent.

—Dr. James Marion Sims, from his autobiography, *The Story of My Life*

Mt. Meigs Arrival

It's the most city I've ever seen.
When we ride up to the big-house,
the land has all the things I know:
honeysuckles, pines
unseen crickets off somewhere,
and the air is the same sweet I've known my whole life.

But I don't see a cotton field.
The doctor offered his hand
when I stepped down from the carriage
and onto his land.
So much need between our hands,
the azaleas face open to summer.

The Doctor Asks If I Want to Go Home the Way I Came

Mt. Meigs, Alabama, June 1845

The first day is the worst. He rolls his sleeves up slow, cuffs white and crisp as gardenias. He says to lift my skirts up higher—*roll them up around your waist*, he says. He drapes a white sheet over the table. I climb up and crouch on my knees and hands, like Delia showed me, kneeling deeper when his naked fingers press the middle of my back. His cold hand makes my spine shiver and he tells me *you're gonna have to learn to keep still*. My behind is high up in the air. Naked as the day I was born, like when that overseer turned my skirts up over my head to give me lashes. I just sit up there on that table and cry. Next thing you know, I'm sittin' there snifflin' and in walks a pack of white men. I jerk up, clawing at the sheet on the table and pulling down my skirts. The doctor's eyes meet mine, and then he points from my hem to my waist, tells me *this is purely scientific*. A few men place their handkerchiefs over their noses. *Excuse the odor, gentlemen,* he says. Seems like tears were coming up out of a well. One man holds my shins while the doctor puts his tool in. Another stretches me apart. I sure cried that first time, I tell you.

Today the Doctor Says He Will Be Gingerly

And I don't know what that means.

I think my mama knows cause one day
she said she used it in a pie.

One day she came in smelling sweet
after she cooked all day and I said,
What is that?

Butter, she says. Cinnamon, she says. And ginger—
all for a sweet potato pie.

If I could loll in it all now,
In the orange forget sweetness of a pie,
what I would give for it.

Wool Door

Delia is the one who knows it all.
She's the one sidling, idling in the door.
She peeps, her face dry as brown wool
until the doctor tells her
run for fresh water, or hold a piece of woman open.

They cut me open
like a great watermelon.
I am ripe and yellow-bellied
and black seeds crack in their mouths.

Delia knows—Delia has all the secrets.
She was here long ago,
plantin' seeds in the doctor's mind.

Delia in the osnaburg dress,
Delia in the indigo,
Delia is the one who knows.

The odor from this saturation permeated everything, and every corner of the room; and of course, her life was one of suffering and disgust. Death would have been preferable. But patients of this kind never die; they must live and suffer.

—Dr. James Marion Sims

A Thousand Cats

Arrange yourself across the range
of the line, between
him self and *your* self
s p r a w l
for him, well, for you
more open

Don't listen to the smell—
it's just the smell of a thousand cats

arranged in a triangular puss
hissing their hisses through yawn-open
kissers, widemouthed
as you should be

Fold up frog-like
like you want to spring
into another life
let him carve you out
another life

Unfolded

the closer
he comes
I ball my fists
tight.
if I could ball my body up
this tight
he'd never pull me
apart.
he'd never
eye what
I've never
seen myself.

To Bear Witness

Delia held my hand all through it—
my nates splayed open

and like the butcher's meat,
I belonged to that steel.

The doctor standing
in the triangle between like

he always was.
He is the air there

and he will separate the day from the night.
Then the pain

until I see the cow with no head.
I swear it was just as real as you and me;

it walked in *this here* room   hooves clicking,
a black soot hole for a neck.

And now, Delia squeezes my hand to the bone
like the cow is hers,

like it is her spine on the table,
her chattering un-intelligibles

and writhing
all through it.

Belonging

After such intrusion, to whom does the body belong?
                    —Hux Nichols, *Saints and Temples*

she used to feel there
trail her palm over the skin of her right hip
towards the familiar patch of fur
rough as a boar brush
opening her soft parts
yielding
like a folded flower
or some other living thing
worth tenderness

worth tenderness
some other living thing
like a folded flower
yielding
opening her soft parts
rough as a boar brush
to the patch of fur
from her right hip
trailing her palm
she used to feel there

Delia

While they laying up and ailin', the doctor tells me to only give 'em a pinch of biscuit and a sip of water. *Not too much water,* he says. (He don't want them peein' up and messin' up stitches.)

The patient is not cured so long as there is the involun-
tary loss of a single drop of urine.

—Dr. James Marion Sims

So Familiar He Is with Parting Her Brown Legs

Again, as if praying. On my knees. Hands locked together in petition. My body rocks with his prods, his moves. *Still as you can, Anarcha,* he says. The bowls of two pewter spoons are pushed in my body, yet they are kinder than his hands. He names it *speculum.* I lean my left wall against the left spoon, away from the wound. I believe this time I will bear it. His hands. He begins stitching with strips of catgut. Some moans curve into wails, saturating the wooden walls with something that won't wash out. His frustration cuts the air between us. Then his wife is calling his name. The spoons are quickly pulled out, a quick suck that leaves me breathless. He tells me he will bring back silk to stitch me, after lunch. I uncurl dizzily on the bed. I no longer bother to cover up.

Days before the dead fetus came by forceps. Worked into the vagina, the metal shifted for its own comfort, then clamped around the infant's head, dragged itself and the stiff corpse down the vaginal walls. So much force that the wall between the canal and anal cavity was severed, leaving an open wound in the vagina. Blood for days—from the uterus, still leaking afterbirth and tissue—the tears, heavy trauma, as yet unstitched, allowing urine to pool in the vaginal canal, creating an odor unbearable to the senses, though even with this, soon the doctor is able to perform the surgeries unmasked, undaunted, so familiar he is with parting her brown legs and shifting his weight between, between, the odor filling the space that separates them, binding them together when it enters his nostrils like a battling ghost.

Dog in the Hospital

There's suffering here—
all of us spilling and moaning it

The dog trots in, darting
between pine sickbeds to catch a fly

We are stiff to make him forget us,
we hold our breath,
wish him more flies for distraction

He still nudges his cool nose into my kneecap,
licks at my calf
If I were able,

I would rise up shivering in this heat,
I would kick that dog in his eyes and all down his nose,
I would kick him bloody and yelping out the door

Sometimes I Think I Should Have Stayed Where I Was At

I thought the world ended at the tree line behind the cottonfield. I didn't know there was any more to it than that.

Fresh Sheet

1

White Lake
keeping the crease she pressed in
when it first came out of the sun

he no longer talks,
just waves his hand towards the table

I lay myself in the center,
part like the red sea—

I drift

II.

My patients are all perfectly satisfied with what I am
doing for them.

—Dr. James Marion Sims

Oak, Pine, Basswood

Mt. Meigs, AL, Present Day

in mt. meigs, fields of ugly cotton plants persist,
their bolls colded over and forever done, afflicting the stalks
like boils, a mutated offspring of their ancestors

which were *so carefully*
tended, every year new seeds sewn, the land then rife with surety
and always turned with the best

dung which yielded a most white and beautiful—
cotton flower

blossoming now are the ones who refuse to die,
this kind never die,
they must live and suffer.

Silk Umbrella, Dancing Pumps

Mt. Meigs, AL, Present Day

my unique questions are referred to mary catherine, reference
queen of the mt. meigs library

as she enters, mary catherine smiles her knowledge about the dr.
yes, she knows—
per usual, she's arrived right on time

she tucks her wet umbrella into a corner and the rain
she's brought inside
runs down the all-weather wings of it, pools onto the library floor

hardly breathing she leads me to a book on the history of mt.
meigs:

*He's famous because he operated on an African American
woman and saved her life!*

Mary Catherine Is a Defeathered Chicken

She's the cool squish-bird in plastic
wrap. Today she wears her own hair,
a mush brown

helmet wig. But there is something pure
about her, something as demure-soft

as her shoes. I imagine
her feet wrapped in that leather, tender buffed sheep—

bare feet—
how the heel and ball roll, lay, get

up again—leisurely, as if they were made
for a chaise,

I imagine her feet so soft in my hands,
I could bone squeeze them crushed.

wild and forbidding

marycatherine=historical preservation society of mt. meigs.
marycatherine *loves* landmarks.
She says she knows where the doctor's house is. She gives me
three sets of directions: *go to the light, make a right, when you
come to the post office, make another, it's two or three houses
down on the left* (what's found instead are storage units and
cleared land.) I drive back to the library. *Well, on the right, then,
if there are houses on the right. The house is overgrown, you
probably can't see it from the road.* Back in the car, I turn to the
right and drive into a path cut in a forest, it was all a forest, then
suddenly: an emu! Tall and staring, frightening—its long neck
and beaked eyes pierced straight at me—its feathers like ash. My
body is all pause and flight, I press the gas my way out of there.

I can't seem to get to mt. meigs

Maybe if I leave early in the morning, so early it is still dark, I could arrive and see the sunrise over what I know will be abandoned fields. I could stay and write for two hours and drive my way home. I wouldn't miss the day with my children. I can't miss a day, and this is stopping me from writing the book. A woman in Montgomery tells me she's never heard of Mt. Meigs, but she thinks it's out on Eighty-Two. *Isn't Mt. Meigs down off Eighty-Two?* Her eyes weighing me. Her eyes crossing over my face, the baby in my arms, wondering.

III.

Prayer Meeting

Way after night has put on his robe,
we put the washpot to the door
to catch our voices.

In the middle of all the shouting
and praising is the prettiest black boy
with big cow eyes

and my heart
sets to beating like a drum.
Folks laid out on the ground,
slain in the spirit
and all I see is this boy:

he has the straightest string of pearls
for teeth.

The Orange

He says don't worry about where he got it from
His hand at my belly—my baby's whole world in his palm

Eat this orange for the baby
go on, take it for my baby

His pine needle face to my face,
orange sections burst in our mouth
His words burn a hole in my dress:
We're stealin' sweet water, girl,

and it is sooo sweet
He says more things I won't tell you—
until something warm, like honey,
fills my cup

Overseer Story (Told with a Smile)

Laugh while the years
race
down your face.
> —Maya Angelou, "Why Are They Happy People?"

He dug a hole in the ground
in the shape of my big belly,

laid me across it,
then commenced
to laying on the lashes.

The whole time he beat me,
felt like my heart was gon' bust,
and what with the little one

kickin' my insides,
while he beat my outsides,
I thought I was gon' die.

I swear, I thought I was gon' die!

Delia

The morning I was born my mama carried me to an oak tree to let it nurse me while she went back to the fields.

Elegy for a Stillborn

To the One Who Carries Him Away

All of my children have died or wandered away.
        —Molly Ammonds, *from a 1937 slave narrative interview*

Here are the milk and songs from my breast.
Here is his cover sewed from calico scrap
and dyed with peachtree.
Take this for nights when he is cold.

Here is the sheet I stole soap for
and washed in secret,
to catch him when he came.
It was to give him a clean start.

Take the old dresser drawer I meant for a cradle.
You will need pins from the washwoman
and this wrap from my hips—
You can carry him against your back.

Take the knife from under my bed
that they used to cut the pain.
I did not make a basket of medicines
I did not want to mark him sick,

But here is pine-top tea, and elderbrush.
Here are mullen leaves for when he cuts teeth.
Here is his corn husk doll.
And take the place I prepared for him near the fire:

the quilt folded in half, then again
so he would rest against something soft.
Take the room full of times
my hand crossed over my belly,

a prayer on my lips.

Southern Pastoral

little black children
march baskets of big-house
linens to the washwoman's
shadow in the field

a blonde baby whimpers
from the green grass floor

the washwoman sways over the pot of lye,
her movements careful to not disturb
the fresh wounds in her back
she slowly works in soiled
linens with a soaked wooden stick

the silver-faced surface
winks at her in the sunlight

a wind starts up and lifts tufts
of the baby's hair
the baby's cotton
cheeks flush red

he begins to cry
and crawl towards the washwoman, who leans
the wet stick against the pot's belly

the baby reaches her hem, salt
tears on his face, salt
on her back

she lifts him into the air

for seconds he is framed by the blue sky
the rush of her smell clouds through his nostrils

then quietly, as if told to
hush, the hungry lye opens
and closes its mouth

The Milk Still Comes In

milk breasts
mushroomed plump
like hoecakes baked in ashes

they always hold milk,
like the cloud-water when a dandelion stem
is broken.

milk veins dressed in breasts.
I press the teat for milk—
milk meant for a little, lost, baby.

they'd said when it came I'd feel a tingle,
but it was as sure as a citrus press,
inside I felt a hand clutch a handle

to pull it in.
my breasts—lump-full
with milk that never sours,

now given to little unknown mouths
that draw relentlessly, spoiling
what was meant to be hers.

Delia

All I can say is: my mind is gone off somewhere else. I mix hot lard to keep the ghosts away but they still come—they come carrying my breasts. One breast in each hand, like justice.

I Could Never Disremember the Fireflies

I caught fireflies for hours in the evenings
with my girl-cousin, Irene.
I can see us now,
just running around in our bare feet
while the stars turn on
and off.

Sometimes when we cupped a firefly,
we'd catch a bit of blue night with it too.

We had to peel the evening off the firefly
before we could put it in the jar.

Moon

If I was up there with you
I'd dress yellow all the time
and some nights I'd wear copper like you

If I could get up there with you
I'd forget all about this life
Leave the earth the way you did
a long, long time ago

Just Like the Light of God

The Lord is surely the one who's been with me all this time. I was just like a motherless child, but the Lord, the mother to the motherless—has been the only one right here with me, all this time.

I've Got Life

What I've got
is calves and heels to carry me
and this heart that only God can stop.

I've got these fingers
to snap in time.

I've got this behind for sitting,
so I don't sit on my spine.

I've got these shoulders only I can shrug,
breasts that letdown when I get the feeling,
and a bird neck that carries my head and all my blood—

These lips only move if *I* tell them to, if *I* want them to.
There is so much my body can still do.
Plus, I've got these eyes for watching you.

I am perfectly content, and nothing could induce me to leave Montgomery. I have no ungratified ambition or desire.

—Dr. James Marion Sims

What Yields

This poem is a sonnet corona of eleven modified sonnets, all directly addressing the doctor and his motives for experimentation. The speaker is Anarcha, who endured thirty surgeries. Sims used opium, which he only administered after the surgeries, to keep his subjects subdued and for pain. In addition to providing pain relief, opium contributes to memory loss and confusion, effects which are reflected in these sonnets.

I

The day we were born, we belonged to you.
These clay-sculpted women—yours. There is no
respite to offer—such exquisite wrongs
remain. Our vulvas: the future you wrote

against the back of your hand. Born to be
seen by you, we are the bodies you
strive against. The triangle axis gleams.
It is June, your glinting silver blade new—

you—slick as butter. So yours, we wonder
if the saliva in our mouths is still
ours. We're denied water to protect sutures.
My parched tongue circles for wisps

of spit. You could leave me this one thing. Thief,
all night you drink water from my body.

II

All night you drink water from my body.
You sneak from your bed, taking the worn way
towards the wood shack over the chickweed
and white clover. We call it shack. You say,

hospital. You stop bedside, and full of
need you straddle me, squat down, your haunches
hovering low, graze my throbbing vulva.
You claw the back of my neck so my head

falls aside like a pansy, then you call
for the water in my body to rise.
Come up, you sing. Dizzied and stunned I watch
it rising like so many beads of wine.

In the mornings I am bare. I am shut.
I am dead where I lie, already plucked.

III

I am dead where I lie, already plucked.
Yet all afternoon, sir, I have risen
up out of this whiteness—out of its touch
I come and though my mind is dim

I will say no, split your trembling lip by
my refusal. I've been longing to see
the rush of blood to your mouth, your pink lie
distended, the flush of blood to your cheeks.

I've been reaching for the surface to show
what my fists can do. My eyes reach for you
out of reach. I am too much to feel, too
impossible to be known. All afternoon

you slept in down, snug against your wife's dove back.
Bodies above virtue are never black.

IV

Bodies above virtue are never black.
Sprawling dewberries grow along your fence;
since most days we are hungry, we take
them—fill hemp sacks we hide against our hips.

When each bite unravels in our mouths
we imagine a sweeter history
and more hope than you could ever allow.
Desperate, we gorge on dewberries—

the heady berries and our molars' slow
grinding drown out the distant cries of
thief. Crushed berry over berry over
berry, this joy—the closest thing to love.

Sated, we hide the blue-stained sacks again.
Our eyes blink back the river to be lost in.

V

Your eyes blink back the river to be lost in
You clutch your elbows, pacing the sickroom
walled with basswood, eleven beds sinking
like monuments into a red clay floor.

Our bodies taut in their sheets, locked in place,
calculating your restraint. We keep our
breath, waiting. Then you begin your complaint:
we aren't *trying* to heal. Unchecked urine

in our wet beds instead of the waste pail.
Piss compromises the stitches and we
know it. And how many times must you tell
us to lie still? You leave us. There will be

no dosage today. The held cries lift.
First, you'd have to consider us women.

VI

First, you'd have to consider us women,
realize our hearts beat under the bush.
You'd have to think my heart longed like yours
And that my mind wasn't mindless, awash

with nothing. I am a hot quaking body—
prime material subject. To you,
I am only worth what can be gleaned.
And you would have to know I meet the pain

how your wife would: imagine *her* blushed pink
frame, gap-legged like a birth-slick colt, quaking.
But you cannot hold both of us in mind
at once. My ability to bear is

immeasurable. Pain discriminates.
Material subject—I am rabbit.

VII

Material subject. I am rabbit.
I skitter the path to crooked river,
scratch up the perfect stones and carry them
to my litter and when they clamor to nurse—

Their soft seeking nostrils nudging my teats—
I beat their bodies, stoned against the rocks
I trample, crush red skulls, dash. Panting
blood into the grass, their buff fur bodies

set in an array of poses, the weeds
bowed down, draining blood that will not cry out.
My babies sink into the ground, drowning.
I am only fit to be without.

I swallow the last stones. Your shadow looms.
Now, the whole earth has turned to look at you.

VIII

Now, the whole earth has turned to look at you.
And we see the gray hairs curling out of
your nose. We nod off like pine trees as you
stitch. Always sighing, you hover

over us. Fool, we know you will never
be done, though you *promise promise promise*
it will work this time. We've grown wiser
to your kindness. We watch you thread our missed

days and nights. Your needle unmends our seams.
Silk? Catgut? You should have known the catgut
would fester. How careless can you be?
Did your dumb mama drop you dumb? You smug

reckless thief. The whole earth can hear you breathe.
Even the clouds agree: we're dead where we sleep.

IX

Even the clouds agree: we're dead where we sleep.
Between sleep and waking my gaze follows
yours as you scan the room of destiny.
Picking through the moss of your mind so

carefully, you decide who you will heal
today. Your hair has grown gray right above
the ears, you could be a wren standing near,
shifting foot to foot in the door, nervous.

You pull out the notes from your leather bag,
reading and murmuring through surgeries—
failures, the *almosts* bore against our backs.
Every note marked becomes the symphony

you compose, and yes, we will render it.
We are rotting fruit, yet our bodies yield.

X

We are rotting fruit, yet our bodies yield.
How easily we yield to you, for you.
We slide into our poses, blossoming.
You examine our stalks for blight, mildew

and rust. One morning your eyes examine
the field and we are ripe. Through sixteen
seasons you have tended us, kept us tilled
and well-drained. You've cultivated after each

rain and sewed crimson clover in the rows
between us. Not one boll weevil has stained
our leaves. With care, you have nourished the soil.
And now, the time has come for you to claim

the crop that you've sewn. Your harvest will be.
We must yield, even if you *lie* to reap.

XI

We must yield, even if you lie to reap.
Untuck the lie from the roof of your mouth
and set it free. If you write it, it will be.
It will set right the frown on your wife's

lips, make it worth it. *Is it worth it?*
Her unspoken question, she doesn't see
what wealth can be gained from digging into
an empty woman. She never believed

it was mending when she heard wails sound
their way up to the house, *sounds like rabbits
dying* she'd said, but never fixed her mouth
to help us. Write history, it will be.

Try out the words in your mouth. We're healed.
The day we were born we belonged to you.

Invention

duck-billed speculum fashioned
on the backs of swans—

all the furious flurry
beneath

IV.

Blueberry Poem

for Terence Crutcher

Write a poem about blueberries, they said—
how cold and sweet and stolen.
Write that poem instead of the poem
I carry in my chest as I move down the sidewalk,
the poem breathing and growing with every step, stretching
toward—

Write a poem about blueberries
instead of the one about the body, which is tender,
crushed in the road, and leaking blue.
How easily the crushed pulp
disperses with the rain.

Write a poem about blueberries;
how they grow low to the ground
or reach up over fences,
for relief.

Write this poem instead of the mother's grief
over the membrane torn in her son's mouth,
his last word, "oh"
The shape of a blueberry.

Meeting Anarcha

Present Day

Anarcha in my garden
is thoughtful:
her eyes
take in the once flowers
twisted in death poses

Her nose twitches
as honeybees descend onto the salvia,
then whiz past us to carry stripped pollen
toward hives somewhere deep
in the woods

She tells me about hives,
honeybees her mother tended,
about the taste of their hard-won fruit,
and how even bees
got to see the fruit of their labor
If I were a bee,
I wouldn't want to give my honey
away neither

She can't believe the *time*
we have to sit here:
me, holding my bowl of Lucky Charms,
she, holding her left hand
in her right, a small collection

In the canopy of leaves and limbs
above cicadas beep and buzz
like ready ovens,
sounding off and filling our silence

Across the years, the cicadas never stop

The spider's thread—carelessly tethered—
flies off in the shyest of breezes

and suddenly I know, all I know
must do a kind of giving up,
a letting go

Brief, Terrific Rainstorms

what the egret regrets; what the wolf duck loves:
frightening women roaming the woods for blackberries,
persimmons, hickory nuts

bite the pine tree, bark rot granules,
molar pestle—this is what bitter is:
feet in the black earth black
berries wilding from the ground
live fingers wound severely around the fruit

For Dorothy Lorena Davis

It opens in black and white:
my seventeenth summer,
Eight Mile, Alabama.

I was dancing an old dance deep
in my grandmother's arms.
That cymbal summer

I wore a maroon dress
I'd be grounded for wearing—
like a second skin.

Those red dust days in Eight Mile were so hot
people stopped saying it was hot.
        We all smelled like outside.

My grandmother—not subtle with love—
made saucepans of Cream of Wheat,
the right amount of butter stirred in.

I didn't really know
how to take the love.
With a grain of salt?

Eight Mile: the rotted oak that still held
        three tire swings,
            vulture always eating the remains of a dog.

My grandmother,
       a warm habitation,
              a lemon pound cake baked.

Her Knife

Elegy for Dorothy Lorena Davis

What still cuts is her Blackwood-handled knife—
the steel blade thin and water-stained, aged yet sharp.
She used it for the pork she pierced to make pockets for garlic
cloves.
It took nearly an hour to peel the flaky suits
from the cloves, wispy like onion peel, falling aside
on the counter beneath her hands,

which were softer than anything I've touched—
they broke nothing, held much.
One day she offered me part of her yellow apple,
held out a slice against the side of the knife, and I refused, though
I wanted it.
She frowned, her soft nails clutching the heel of her palm,
threatening a punch and then laughing it open.

If a clove sought its way out of the pork, slipping out like a white
fish fighting a hook,
she'd turn the knife's blade on its side, prod the head of the clove
until it gave, moved back into the meat.
This was the only knife she used.
I saw it cut the pork on-the-grain—
she never needed a man around to cut meat.

The knife sliced slivers of her decadent pound cake.
This paring knife, the only utensil she never put away,
its home in the dish drain beside the sink.

The blade opened everything except her skin;
even if a thumb braced against it while cutting
it would not nick her skin,
an unspoken agreement of tenderness between knife and woman.

This Poem Resists with Joy

Hearing her own sky-blue vowels resound
then return across the clearing, Vivienne
is finally sated. Not told—here in the green photo
of her papa's wooded land—to shush,
be quiet, or the neighbors—
Now, her bell voice echoes
high-pitched snippets of "Row Your Boat"
unhindered by suburb or road. My little redbird.
She lies on her back on the trampoline,
her white breath coming in pants.
I want to adequately describe her here:
her fuzzy cornrowed head resting,
small body relaxed against the black top of the trampoline
her papa scrubbed clean just that morning.
All day the soapy bed dried in an uncommon January
marked with sunlight and excessive spring.
I want you to see her butterscotch face, ruddy from leaps,
breath reaching the clouds, eyes
wondering.

Teeth

for Eden, Vivienne & Maya

This body housed three women,
accommodated three sets of fists,
six eyes and three belly buttons.
It allowed iron bones and spines
to raise their way into existence.

This morning my right breast stretched
from my robe, touched my infant's mouth,
bobbed like branches over a water
until her sharp fish mouth closed onto it;
her lips as imperceptible as a cat's,
her lips as thin.

I am grateful to this constellation
for healing itself *again*,
for sealing off blood, its vessels,
for scarring to create a second row of stars
to run my right fingers over, lighting them with heat
as they travel across—

My Mother Bathes Me after I Give Birth

for Wanda Marie Ravenell

Washing my collapsed belly, crossing the soapy cloth over my
wilted shoulders and back is a familiar act for my mother, and
washing her child is like riding a bike, a thing she will not forget.

At first I feel something as deep as shame, standing naked and
framed by the backsplash of the shower, the remnants of the
anesthesia clattering through me.

I watch the blood pool between my feet before narrowing as it
moves toward the drain. My shoulders can no longer support the
weight of my mind. I can only look at the tiled shower floor and
not at any part of my mother's face.

My babies have been taken straight to the NICU from my body.
I kissed unfeeling kisses on their lips and faces, and before the
kisses dry, they are swaddled tight and wheeled away. I am
bleeding from their exit, my incision numb yet throbbing at the
belly.

The nurse has said to allow the water to soak the bandage, and it
will fall off the incision. It does. While my mother soaps my arms
I wash between my legs with another cloth, astounded at the
blood. I glance at my mother what to do with the reddened cloth,
she says, *let it fall in the tub.*

Moments later a heap of soaking cloths near the drain. My
mother has asked for extra towels—warm towels, and she wraps

them around me when I've stepped out of the shower. She dries me with the door shut to keep the heat in. When she moves the lotion over my skin with her hands I breathe. I am an aching shell but her touch says I am worth tenderness.

Acknowledgments

First, all my love and gratitude to my parents, Rick and Wanda Ravenell, who have always believed.

A heartfelt thank-you to my Muffin and great love, Marcus Monté Maples. Thank you to my daughters, Vivienne, Eden, and Maya, for being poetry and my reasons to be bold. My sibs: Nijon, Natylie, Nick, and Kayna, for the love and laughter and for being my people. Thank you to Grandma Mena. Thank you to Uncle Carl, Uncle James, Uncle Link, Uncle Larry, Uncle Marvin, Uncle Juney, Uncle Errol, Uncle Kenny, and Aunt Barb. All of my love to Jade Washington—we miss you. Thank you to my cousins for always being an example: Vernon, Rodney, and Wayne. I love you all. Thank you to the Reed family for your always-kindness. Sis Beverly Mellix for teaching me. Chantell Limerick, for your brain being friends with my brain. Daron Drew for being my ride-or-die and road-dog. Paula, for being my roommate all those years ago and for "considering" doing it again. I love you and thank you for loving me. Thank you to Javacia Bowser for See Jane Write and always pushing me into the deep end of the pool. Thanks to all of the librarians from my K–12 education. Issiah Byrd for telling me I could be a writer. Arron Williams for making me believe it. And to my mentors, who gave me things I could never name—Abraham Smith, Joyelle McSweeney, and Joel Brouwer—I could never thank you enough. A heartfelt thank-you to my grandmother, Dorothy Lorena Davis, who would have loved to see this, but knew it was coming. Thank you to the wonderful folks at the Rockefeller Brothers Foundation, who provided the space where this work began. Thank you to the voices of Cave Canem that always say, *tell the stories for those who can't.* Thank you to the individuals who were the first readers and editors of this manuscript: Erin Lyndal Martin, Joel Brouwer, Ashley Jones, T. J. Beitelman, Robert Ricardo Reese, and Abraham Smith. (A special thanks to my colleagues and friends, Ashley and T. J.) Thanks to the University Press of Kentucky and series editor Lisa Williams for seeing the value of this work and giving me an opportunity to share it. Above all else, I thank God for giving me great ideas, specifically the idea for the sonnet corona. Thank you! Thank you for being everything I need and always "doing a new thing."

Thanks to the editors of the following journals in which these poems, sometimes in different versions, first appeared:

Bayou Magazine: "Her Knife" (2018).

Berkeley Poetry Review: "Blueberry Poem" (issue 47, 2017, https://www.ocf.berkeley.edu/~bpr/47th-issue/).

Birmingham Arts Journal: "For Dorothy Lorena Davis" (vol. 14, issue 1, Fall 2017).

Obsidian: Literature and Arts in the African Diaspora: "The Milk Still Comes In" and "Teeth" (vol. 43.2, 2018).

Open Letters Monthly: "This Poem Resists with Joy" (Spring 2017, https://www.openlettersmonthly.com/this-poem-will-resist-with-joy/).

PLUCK! Literary Journal: "To Bear Witness," "Elegy for a Stillborn."

Puerto del Sol: "So Familiar He Is with Parting Her Brown Legs" (2018).

Track\\Four Journal: "Mary Catherine Is a Defeathered Chicken" (vol. 1, issue 1, Spring 2016, http://www.trackfourjournal.com/kwoya-fagin-maples-v1i1.html).

"Belonging" appeared in the Cave Canem digital chapbook anthology, *Gather Round 2014.*

"Southern Pastoral," "I've Got Life," and "The Doctor Asks If I'd Like To Go Home the Way I Came" appeared online in *Southern Women's Review* (2018).

"What Yields" appeared in *Blackbird Poetry Review* and a special issue of *Obsidian: Literature and Arts in the African Diaspora* (vol. 43.2, 2018) as a finalist for the 2017 Gwendolyn Brooks Centennial Poetry Prize.

Notes

The dedication of this book is adapted from lines from "Fever 103°" by Sylvia Plath.

"Delia" was a house slave, according to Sims's letters. She was not an experimental subject, but she was certainly a witness and aide.

In south Alabama, some women call their vaginas "cats."

Epigraphs on pages 5, 10, 16, 23, and 45 are direct quotes from James Marion Sims's autobiography, *The Story of My Life*.

The epigraph for "Overseer Story (Told with a Smile)" is from Maya Angelou's poem, "Why Are They Happy People?"

The "Elegy for a Stillborn" epigraph by Molly Ammonds is from a 1937 interview by Gertha Couric, *Federal Writers' Project: Slave Narrative Project, Vol. 1, Alabama, Aarons–Young, 1936–1937*. Washington, DC: Library of Congress, https://www .loc.gov/item/mesn010/ (accessed March 23, 2018).

"Overseer Story" and "Southern Pastoral" include direct references to slave narratives from *Voices of Slavery: 100 Authentic Slave Narratives,* edited by Norman R. Yetman.

The title "Just Like the Light of God" comes from a lyric in the gospel spiritual, "Keep Your Lamp Trimmed and Burnin'," in a version of the song sung by Irene Williams, which was procured by the Federal Writers' Project. A recording of Williams's rendition is archived on the Library of Congress website, www.loc.gov.

"What Yields" was written in response to the concept of the "medical plantation" discussed in Harriet Washington's book, *Medical Apartheid: The Dark History of Medical Experimentation on Black Americans from Colonial Times to the Present.*

Bibliography

Alabama Slave Narratives: A Folk History of Slavery in Alabama from Interviews with Former Slaves. Bedford, MA: Applewood, 2006.

"Born in Slavery: Slave Narratives from the Federal Writers' Project, 1936–1938." Library of Congress, Washington, DC. https://www.loc.gov/collections/slave-narratives-from-the-federal-writers-project-1936-to-1938/about-this-collection/.

Breedon, James O., ed. *Advice among Masters: The Ideal in Slave Management in the Old South*. Westport, CT: Greenwood, 1980.

McGregor, Deborah Kuhn. *From Midwives to Medicine: The Birth of American Gynecology*. New Brunswick, NJ: Rutgers Univ. Press, 1998.

Scott, John B. *Memories of the Mount: The Story of Mt. Meigs, Alabama*. Montgomery, AL: Black Belt, 1993.

Sims, James Marion. *The Story of My Life*. New York: Appleton, 1884.

Slave Narratives: A Folk History of Slavery in the United States from Interviews with Former Slaves. Washington, DC: Library of Congress, 1941.

Washington, Harriet A. *Medical Apartheid: The Dark History of Medical Experimentation on Black Americans from Colonial Times to the Present*. New York: Harlem Moon, 2006.

Yetman, Norman R., ed. *Voices from Slavery: 100 Authentic Slave Narratives*. Mineola, New York: Dover, 2000.

THE UNIVERSITY PRESS OF KENTUCKY
NEW POETRY AND PROSE SERIES

This series features books of contemporary poetry and fiction that exhibit a profound attention to language, strong imagination, formal inventiveness, and awareness of one's literary roots.

SERIES EDITOR: Lisa Williams

ADVISORY BOARD: Camille Dungy, Rebecca Morgan Frank, Silas House, Davis McCombs, and Roger Reeves

Sponsored by Centre College